W9-BQV-222

Published by Jastin Enterprises, LLC

Stock Imagery supplied by iStock, StoryBlocks and Adobe

Any website addresses used in this book are fictitious; however, due to the changing nature of the Internet, the web address characteristics may change since publication.

ISBN-13: 978-1724364944
ISBN-10: 1724364944

Dedication

BUILDING CYBER-READY WORKERS FROM A YOUNG AGE TO MEET NATIONAL WORKFORCE DEMANDS OF THE FUTURE

This book is dedicated to supporting the workforce needs for the 21st century in the areas of cybersecurity. Some surveys estimate that there were over 200,000 cybersecurity jobs left unfilled in 2015 and the demand will grow exponentially over the next 20 years. This book, and subsequent episodes, will educate and inspire a new generation of potential cyber technologists, workers and managers who will have had the opportunity to experience the cybersecurity territory from early childhood, thus making "cyber speak" and careers in this area much less foreign.

The book targets children between the ages of 8 and 12, as well as adults who like to read with them. Everyone can benefit from reading these episodes, to become safer online.

McGarry (2013) reported that General Keith Alexander, former Director, NSA, described cybersecurity work as a "tremendous opportunity for young people…" He said, "This generation is coming up cyber savvy," after explaining how his almost two-year-old granddaughter knows how to use an iPad to watch movies on Netflix. "We can train them. We can educate them."

Source: McGarry, B. (Oct. 14, 2013). NSA Chief: What Cyberwarrior Shortage?

ACKNOWLEDGMENTS

To all my friends, family, colleagues and supporters of this effort, I thank you dearly.

~ and ~

To Roy, who fully supported all my ideas with kindness, respect and endless love.

You may have read in the earlier episodes

of Super Cybersecurity Grandma that Jastin, her grandson, is 12 years old and is a very active child on the Internet. Last time we met, Jastin's class had Cyber Career Day at School.

The class was very excited to hear about many of the new jobs that you can get in the cybersecurity field. Jobs that allow you to make

BIG money $$$$$ ("Cha-Ching").

It seems that all Jastin's cyber interests came from what he learned from his many escapades with Phishing, Ransomware, Cyber Bullying, the Internet of Things (IoT), and Privacy and Identity Theft...

One day, Jastin and Super Cee Gee (that's what he calls his grandma) were riding their bicycles in the park. It was a beautiful, sunny day with just a few puffy clouds in the sky. Jastin looked at Super Cee Gee and said, "Well, Grandma, I think I am growing up in the cyber world now, thanks to you helping me out with my computer problems." "Yes," said Super Cee Gee. "I think you have come a long way from being online without thinking about the consequences of doing the wrong things like going to bad websites, cyber bullying, and giving out your private information!"

They both laughed so hard, they threw back their heads looking up at the beautiful sky. Jastin turned to Super Cee Gee and, out of the clear, blue sky said, "What is a cloud?" Super

Cee Gee looked puzzled because she was not sure if Jastin meant a cloud in the sky or a cloud in technology terms.

She wanted to believe that he meant technology but he didn't. That didn't stop her though, from telling him about both.

So, quickly, Super Cee Gee said, "A cloud in the sky is the water that is on our land or in the ocean that evaporates into water vapor. The water vapor rises to the sky and turns back into little droplets of water that eventually accumulate and make clouds. There are many different types of clouds in the sky and the names are based on their shapes." Jastin remembered learning something in Science class about cumulus, cirrus and the many other types of clouds.

Super Cee Gee could not wait to talk to Jastin about Cloud Technology. "Jastin," Super Cee Gee said. "Now, you need to learn about how THE CLOUD is used in the technology world." She continued, "You know I would never miss an opportunity to teach you something about computers and security."

"I know that you have heard of storing (uploading and downloading) your music, books, games, pictures or files in the cloud. When we finish our talk today, you will know what that means."

"To really understand THE CLOUD, you need to have a history lesson about how we used and stored information a long, long time ago!"

Smiling and thinking about the "*good ole days*," Super Cee Gee said, "In the 1970's and 1980's, we had huge computers called mainframes.

They were locked in a big room owned by companies that hired specially-trained computer people handling the equipment and the programs that ran on the computers.

Your grandparent's banking and work information was first stored on punched cards.

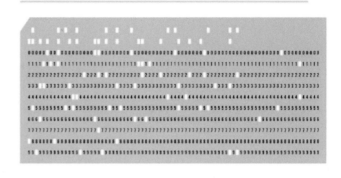

Your contacts were on paper in a big phone book. There wasn't any thought about looking at information on a computer screen, or saving pictures, videos, books and music on computers like we do today. But someone came up with the idea to put all of our computer *stuff* into what is called a database."

Super Cee Gee continued, "...along with the databases came personal computers. These  were the first computers that a regular person could buy for their home or small office and not have to rely on the one person who ran the mainframe. The screens were not very lively or colorful (they were drab, green and gray colors). Another problem, we couldn't really save a lot of *data* or *stuff* on these old machines because they didn't have a lot of disk space.

If you wanted to send a letter or file to someone else, you had to physically walk it over to them (we  called that Sneaker Net – get it?).

As exciting as it was with many people starting to have a computer at home, well, we were still not satisfied. All of us wanted a way to talk to each other with these computers. So, the U.S. Government invented networks to connect computers together all around the whole world. Sneaker Net just was not working!

Along with networking, computer screens got prettier, more colorful, and easy to use.

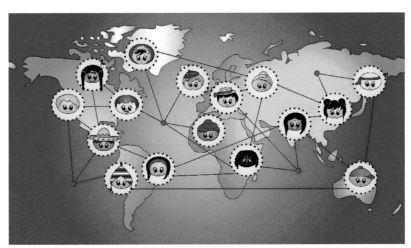 Above all, we got the *World Wide Web*. We now call it The Internet and can use it to talk to everyone in the world and search for all the information we will ever need. The Internet gave us Google ™ other search

engines, apps, and social media where we could make online friends".

Super Cee Gee looked at Jastin and he seemed like he wasn't paying attention, so she fast-forwarded to the 21st century where just about everyone has smart phones and wireless tools, and we don't have to worry about how many disk drives we need for storing our data.

She said, "We can have all of the music, e-mails, texts, books, pictures, files, video games, and  anything else and save it in THE CLOUD. Yeah!!!" Jastin perked up when he heard the words video games. He started to wonder and asked Super Cee Gee, "How did THE CLOUD get its name? It's a weird one."

Super Cee Gee said, "THE CLOUD got its name because when the smart people who were creating computers, apps, networks and other things, needed a way to show, in one picture, how <u>all</u> the many network connections and computers in The Internet stored information.

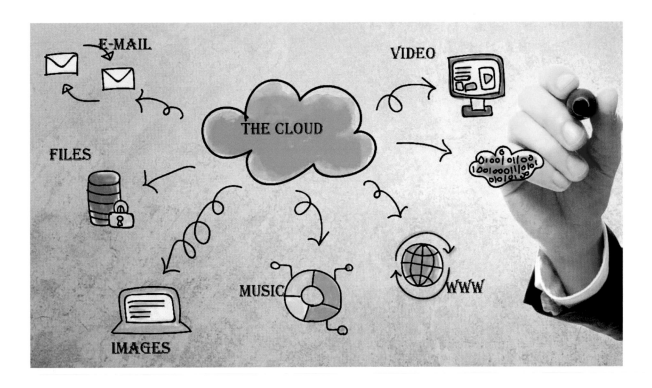

They drew a big cloud to easily show what they were trying to get across. I guess you can say they were being a bit lazy."

Now, Jastin got it. He realized that a real, live CLOUD for computers doesn't exist. It is an idea that you cannot really touch. It is a ginormous number of computers and networks that saves and transports our data so that we can share stuff when we use our tablets, smart phones, video games, smart TVs, Internet of Things devices and computers.

Because the cloud is so large and contains everyone's information  you have to be concerned about cybersecurity in protecting the information and privacy. That requires a lot of work by the "good guy hackers" to keep the "bad guy hackers" out.

So, Super Cee Gee finished telling her story to Jastin about Cloud Computing.

He was fascinated to find out that it was not a real thing that he could actually visit, see, smell or touch. He finally learned what it meant to 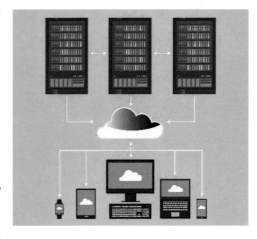 upload and download information to THE CLOUD, how powerful it was and how it is an easy way for him to use technology – much different from the olden days.

Jastin also recalled what he learned at Cyber Career Day at his school. He asked Super Cee Gee, "So, are there new jobs created because of THE CLOUD?" Super Cee Gee said, "There are many jobs for people who work with

THE CLOUD - Again, there are those high-paying jobs like managing The Cloud, Cloud privacy experts, Cloud network technicians, Cloud salespeople, Cloud designers and many, many more – with special emphasis on the Cloud Security Experts!

Well, as the day went on, the real clouds opened up and started to rain. Super Cee Gee and Jastin were okay with it, as they now knew how real clouds form, and most of all, it was still a happy day because Jastin learned something new and important to him, growing up in the world of technology.

Glossary

Apps – Software programs that run on mobile devices to allow you to play games and music, read printed and audio books, and for business transactions like banking, Uber, and checking on your accounts, and for working in social media like Facebook, Twitter, Snapchat. Users download (usually from The Cloud) and install Apps on their devices. The term App is short for Applications.

Bits and Bytes – Bits and Bytes are somewhat complicated terms but the easiest way to describe them is to say that they are how your information is passed along on computers, wires and computer networks. When you learn more about computers and communications, you will see data is sent in 0s and 1s along the network which is the "language" that computers understand. The real computer "geeks" like studying this level of computer concepts. For many cybersecurity-related jobs, you do not need to know this level of detail.

Cloud Technology (THE CLOUD) – The cloud is a picture model that we use for explaining the many computers, network, cables, routers in the world that help us – the users of computers and mobile devices – to communicate and share files. The Apps and data reside in the cloud for easy access from anywhere in the world, at any time.

Cyberbullying – This term is often used to describe many undesirable activities and behaviors related to the Internet, social media, e-mail and texting. The term is derived from traditional bullying in schools, where children were threatened and mistreated in various ways. With so much use of the Internet now, the bullying activities take on a different form, but the negative influences and actions are similar and more pervasive. As such, it has become very difficult to monitor and curtail. Everyone must be aware of this phenomenon so that cyberbullying victims can be protected and cyberbullies can be taught to respect others.

Databases – Databases are a complicated way of storing your files, documents, music, and all the information that describes them. First used in the 1970s, it is now a very sophisticated way of storing information on disk drive hardware. There are special applications and methods of manipulating the information so that it can be presented to you in a sensible way.

Disk Drives – These are the pieces of hardware within a computer that holds (stores) the information the computer needs to perform its duties. Many years ago, disk drives cost a lot of money, so it was expensive to store too much information. Today, disk drives that hold many, many, many files, songs, books, etc. are pretty inexpensive.

Hackers and being Hacked – There are many kinds of hackers - good ones and bad ones. In the past episodes of Super Cee Gee, the focus has been on the hackers who are trying to get into computers, networks, and systems for bad reasons. Hackers can be one person working out of their home or several people in other countries working for large governments. "Black Hat" Hackers use their technology to break into someone else's computer, mostly to steal their information (like credit card information and passwords) to sell to others who buy the information illegally. We have learned about some of the ways (phishing and ransomware) that hackers use to get information for disreputable reasons.

Identity Theft – *Identity* theft happens when a hacker (or anyone else) has enough information about you, like your name, address, social security number, date of birth, school, parents' names, etc. to open bogus accounts in your name. Usually, they create bank accounts or order credit cards that will give them the opportunity to get money – money in your name that YOU may have to pay back. Even if you don't have to pay it back, Identity Theft can ruin your personal reputation. 1-800-IDTHEFT is the number to call for help!

Internet of Things (IoT) - In order to understand IoT, you need to know that computers communicate using "addresses." Every internet device must have this address to be located by another computer. This "Internet Protocol" (IP) addressing scheme is kind of complicated and you can learn more about that later. Today, there are many, many Internet addresses that we can associate with cars, refrigerators, alarm systems, mobile devices, light bulbs, thermostats and other things. Since these "things" can now communicate over the Internet – this term - IoT was coined. IoT is a good thing, and we easily buy and install devices because of the conveniences they provide; but with so many devices talking to each other and possibly sharing personal information, we need to think about some of the cybersecurity dangers.

Internet Privacy – Maintaining your privacy when you are online is a difficult thing to manage. Many people, young and old, freely put personal information in their social media accounts and give it online to companies from which we buy things. Also, as outlined in the Super Cee Gee "IoT" episode, some information is automatically collected by the devices we use. Online users must be vigilant about protecting their personally identifiable information (PII) all the time.

Mainframes – These were the computers that were used long before laptops, personal computers, mobile phones and notebooks. They were able to process lots of information but were only available to big companies and the government. Mainframes required people with special skills to write applications and to run them. They were very powerful for their time, but today, we hold just as much, or more, power and storage in our mobile phones.

Networking – This relates to how computers and all our devices can "talk" to each other. Networks are real, physical pieces of equipment (called servers, routers and switches) connected by cables.

Personal Reputation – Your personal reputation is what you carry with you throughout your life. In the digital world, it includes all the information that exists on the Internet about you: pictures, friends, clubs, school, etc. It includes things that you posted and things that someone else has posted about you. It is important that you only have good things associated with your name and it starts with protecting your privacy and your online personality. As you get older, schools, colleges, and employers will be able to look at your online personal reputation.

Phishing – As a reminder from Jastin's first episode, Phishing attacks are named that because they are just like real fishing where someone throws out the bait on a fishing pole to catch a poor, unsuspecting fish and the fish bites the bait and gets reeled in. Well, in the digital world, hackers often send a bogus e-mail to someone (the bait) hoping that some poor "schmuck" will think it's real and send their precious personal information to them. **Wrong**!

Punched Cards – Before we could communicate with computers with keyboards and mice, it was necessary to use punched cards to provide computers with the instructions to solve a problem. A punched card is made of heavy paper and has holes punched in it in a way that older computers could understand the instructions.

Ransomware – Bad software or (malware) that can stop people from accessing their pc, laptop, tablet or smart phone; in essence, putting a lock on files, pictures, data, contacts, and screens until a ransom is paid to the hacker.

Search Engine – The best way to define a search engine is to give you the examples of the major ones that most people use: Google, Yahoo, and Bing. These are the applications that you use with your browser to search The Internet. You can enter a simple keyword to search for and you will usually get millions of hits.

Sneaker Net – as noted in the story, this is the slang name that was given to the process of sharing files before networks were widely used. If I had a picture on a floppy disk drive that I wanted to give to my friend, I had to walk the disk over to him. With networks, it is as easy as one click or swipe to share files on our computers or smart devices. The name Sneaker Net came about because those were (and still are) what we called tennis shoes.

Social Media – These are the apps that you can use to communicate with anyone in the world. Examples of social media are Facebook, Snapchat, Instagram, and other tools that allow you to have online "friends" with whom you can communicate at any time, any place.

Wireless – when networks were discovered for sharing information among computers, it started out requiring the use of wires (or cables) to hook your device to The Internet or to other computers. Wireless is just what it says. It is a network that allows you to communicate with others without being tethered (tied to) another device. It uses the airwaves to transmit.

Made in the USA
Columbia, SC
10 November 2018